Don Jones' PowerShell 4N00bs

Don Jones

Don Jones' PowerShell 4N00bs

Don Jones

ISBN 9781723812842

Also By Don Jones

The DSC Book

The PowerShell Scripting and Toolmaking Book

Become Hardcore Extreme Black Belt PowerShell Ninja Rockstar

Be the Master

Don Jones' The Cloud 4N00bs

Instructional Design for Mortals

How to Find a Wolf in Siberia

Tales of the Icelandic Troll

PowerShell by Mistake

The Culture of Learning

for the wonderful, supportive, and friendly PowerShell community who've been my friends, colleagues, and inspiration since 2006.

Contents

1. **About this Series** **1**

2. **A Note on Code** **3**

3. **What is PowerShell?** **5**
   What Came Before 7
   Introducing PowerShell 11
   OK - Why Should I Care? 15

4. **Installing PowerShell** **19**
   Windows PowerShell 19
   PowerShell Core 20
   VS Code 21

5. **Your First Console Experience** **23**
   Launch PowerShell 23
   Check Your Version 24
   Run a Command 25
   Files and Folders 26
   Exit 30
   A Good First Step 30

6. **Where Do Commands Come From?** **31**
   Built-In Commands 31
   Comes with Software 33

The Internet . . . 33
PowerShell Gallery . . . 34
Your Own Gallery . . . 37
Seeing What Modules and Commands You Have . 38
What's in a Module? . . . 39
Explore What's Out There . . . 40

7. **How Do I Use This Thing?** . . . **41**
Windows Only: ExecutionPolicy . . . 41
It's Okay to Ask for Help . . . 42
Reading the Help Files . . . 47

8. **Objects and the Magic of Formatting** . . . **53**
Formatting Rules . . . 55
Messing with Objects . . . 58
PowerShell Plays Along . . . 60
Objects: the Important Bits . . . 61

9. **Enter the Pipeline** . . . **63**
Six Pipelines . . . 64
Simple Pipeline Examples . . . 65
Pipeline Input: Plan A . . . 67
Pipeline Input: Plan B . . . 69
Wrapping Up . . . 72

10. **Filtering and Selecting** . . . **75**
Filtering . . . 75
Being Efficient with Filtering . . . 80
Selecting Properties . . . 81
Advanced Selecting . . . 82
Wrapping Up . . . 83

11. **The Very Basics of Scripting** . . . **85**
Wrapping Up . . . 88

12. Going Remote **89**
Enabling Remoting 89
Connectivity 89
Sending Remote Commands 90
Remote Jobs 92
Wrapping Up 93

13. Understanding Your OS **95**

14. The Chapter of Gotchas **99**
Format to the Right 99
ForEach vs. ForEach vs. ForEach 100
Collections vs. Objects 101

15. Where to Next? **103**

16. Welcome to the Community! **105**

1. About this Series

It's always frustrated me that, as technology marches on and becomes more complex, we seem to forget that there's this thing in the world called a "birth rate." Although we constantly have new people being born, growing up, and entering the field, books and other learning materials tend to drop the "total beginner" content over time, focusing on more and more complex and high-end content. So where are the newcomers supposed to learn stuff?

Thus, this series. This is the kind of "evergreen" content that I suspect will change little over time. This isn't a book for someone who's already covered the basics, and it isn't a book for someone looking to become an expert. This is a book for someone interested in getting started, in understanding the core concepts and tasks needed to begin using a technology. It's a book for the "easy stuff" that other experts are bored of talking about.

As I work with other authors to create this content, and as I write myself, my goal is to keep the tone casual and conversational. I want to make this "easy stuff" truly *easy* for you, the reader, to ingest and understand. I want try and give you clear guidance on where to go next, and on what to expect as you go there.

If you're a more-experienced person reading this, you may notice that some of the analogies and comparisons are different from what you're used to. That's because, for the intended audience of this book, I'm not relying on them having an existing knowledge base of the technology to build upon; we're starting from scratch, here, and so I'll be using examples and analogies that are appropriate to that mission. I truly want *anyone* who is familiar with perhaps nothing more than a smartphone to be able to pick this up and do well with it.

I hope you enjoy.

Don Jones, series creator

2. A Note on Code

Formatting computer code for a book can be an enormous pain in the neck. Consider this:

```
Get-Process | Sort-Object -Property VM -Descending \
| Select-Object -First 10 | Format-Table -AutoSize
```

That's meant as one long line of code. But it won't fit in the book, so the backslash character gets used at the end of the overly long line, as a kind of visual "word wrap" character. We realize that this is completely not ideal, but sometimes there's not much we can do about it.

As a result, you'll sometimes see some nasty formatting like that in this book. Other times, we may have truncated the output a bit from what you'd normally see in PowerShell, just to make it fit without the backslashes. We hope you'll understand.

3. What is PowerShell?

If you've used any kind of computer, even that "pocket computer" you call a phone, then you probably have a good idea of how computers work. You click (or tap) icons, you type text into text fields, you drag stuff with a mouse or your finger, and so on. Easy. In the computer world, that's called *using a Graphical User Interface*, although most of us geeks would call it a "GUI" (pronounced, "gooey," like melted chocolate). GUIs are great. Almost anyone can pick up a modern computer and start using it right off the bat, because GUIs kind of make it easier to figure out what you need to do.

The same principle applies if you're working with the bigger computers that run networks, power the Internet, and underpin the cloud. Called *servers* (because they "serve up the goods" to your "client computer"), these expensive machines need people to configure them, install software updates, add new applications, and so on, and GUIs have always made that easy. Need to install updates? Just click the "Updates" button! Easy! Need to change a piece of configuration information, like the network address the computer is reachable at? No problem! Go into the Settings app, click on "Network Settings," and type the correct address into the text box. Easy!

Where GUIs suck is scale. *Scale* is a big thing in the computing industry, and it basically means, "how large can this thing get before it becomes a problem?" Elementary school classrooms, for example, don't scale well. Stick 20 kids in a class and you're probably fine. 25 might be pushing it. 30 starts to feel like a bit too much. By 50, it's all fallen apart and the kids are trying to eat each other, because they've already eaten the teacher.

Scale is important in all kinds of industries. Take cars, for example. Back in the day, before good old Henry Ford came along. Cars were put together by hand. That didn't scale well. If it took 5 guys to build a car, and you wanted to build 10 cars at once, you needed 50 guys. If you wanted 20 at once, you needed 100 guys. Eventually, you ran outta guys. But Henry built machines, so that a car could be built by 2 guys using all the machines â€" and faster, too! And those same 2 guys could build cars all day! Henry increased his scale through *automation.*

GUIs are a bit like those 5 guys building 1 car. If it takes you 5 minutes to complete a task, then it'll take you those same 5 minutes every time you need to perform that task. If you do that task 70 times a day, that's pretty much all you're going to be doing all day. If the business needs that task performed 150 times, you're either going to be putting in a lot of overtime or hiring a friend. And you're both going to end up *really* bored, doing that same task over and over and over and over and over.

So PowerShell is the Henry Ford of computer administration. Instead of clicking buttons and dragging things, you write down what you want the computer to do. You write it down in a kind of language that both you and the computer can understand. Then, when you need the task performed, you just basically point to those instructions, and the computer does it. It does it faster than you, and more reliably, because it never gets bored of doing the same thing over and over and over and over.

What Came Before

This idea of writing down instructions isn't new. Basically, that's what programming is, although when it comes to computer administration, we're talking a super "lightweight" kind of programming, often referred to as *scripting*. Because it's like a movie, right? In a movie, the *script* tells the actors what to say, and often how to move around the set. Computer scripts are the same thing - they tell the computer what to do.

Back in the old days, writing down instructions was the *only* way to tell a computer what do to. GUIs didn't come along, in the server world, until the mid 1990s, and didn't become really common until the late 1990s and early 2000s. Prior to that, everyone just typed whatever they wanted the server to do. Being humans, and being so much better than these mere machines, we typed in *commands*. Commands told the computer what we wanted to do, much like you might command a dog to sit or roll over. You typed these commands into a special app called a *Command-Line Interface*, or CLI. See, it's like the opposite of a GUI. They're both interfaces, or ways of telling a computer what to do; one of them involves typing commands one at a time, and the other involves poking around graphical icons and such.

But commands had two very serious problems, which got worse and worse over time. These are important problems to understand, because they're the two of the exact three things PowerShell was created to solve. And it's also worth mentioning that *puh-lenty* of people don't think these are problems, because they've been working with these problems for so long that they're just used to it. It's like how you never realized how awesome air conditioning was until the first time you experienced it, and then you're like, "um, no, I'll stay inside all summer, thanks." But seriously, lots of folks working on computers don't even think these things *are* problems, but I'll try and make a case that they are, indeed, big bad problems.

Problem One: What Does This Mean?

The first problem is that the commands themselves are weirdly named, weirdly formatted, and really hard to remember until you've been working with them for a decade or so. Like, the learning curve on a common CLI is *massive*. It's people who learn this stuff when they're in college (when your brain is still spongey) and keep doing it all their lives who love these commands; nobody else does. Check it out:

```
ps -A | grep httpd | xargs -n1
```

Clear as mud, right? That's the "language" you had to learn to tell a computer what to do, and in many, many, many places, that's still how you do it. The fact that this is a problem doesn't mean people don't still do it! But this is a problem because it makes it *really hard* for someone else to get into the industry. We realize how that sort of provides job security for the people already in it, but it's terrifying for businesses, who worry that their 60 year-old server admin will leave or die, and they won't be able to find someone else to manage everything.

Problem Two: Connecting Dots

Let's take a look at that command-line example again:

```
ps -A | grep httpd | xargs -n1
```

Now, we want to explain this, because there's an important thing going on, but don't feel you need to *learn* this. What's happening here is a command called `ps`, which gets a list of all the apps the computer is currently running. The `-A` part is a *flag*, or *switch*, which flips the command to a specific behavior. In this case, it means we want to see *all* the apps (called *processes*) running on the computer.

> Next, you see a pipe character: `|`. This means that we don't want to actually see the output of the `ps` command. Rather, we want to *pipe it* to the next command, named `grep`. Think of this as a literal pipe, like a piece of plumbing, connecting the "out" of the first command to the "in" of the second command. So the `grep` command sucks in all the process information, and it looks for lines of text containing `httpd`, because that's what we told it to do. Only those lines get "out" of `grep`, and they're piped, in turn, to the `xargs` command, which does something else with the information.

The *pipe* is the important part, here. It's the idea that one command's output can be used by another command. Stringing them all together lets us achieve some powerful results, such as shutting down just the process named `httpd`, which is what the above command-line does. The *problem* here is that traditional commands just produce these enormous wedges of text as output. For example, here's a bit of what `ps` outputs if you just run it by itself:

```
PID  TTY          TIME CMD
5763 pts/3    00:00:00 zsh
8534 pts/3    00:00:00 ps
```

Charming stuff, right? In reality, almost no other command can do anything with that output as-is. That's why you almost always wind up having to manipulate it, using commands like `grep`, `sed`, and `awk`, before sending it on to another "real" command. And incidentally, I'm picking on the Linux operating system here, but Windows and other operating systems are guilty of the exact same thing in their own CLIs.

And here's the real bummer: suppose you've spent time developing a command-line that is *really* sweet. You're running a command, grabbing its output, looking for specific characters in columns 30 through 35 of each line, and for the lines that match what you want, you're outputting just column 1 through 5, and then sending that on to another command to do something with the info. It's slick, it took a long time to get right, and you're ready to go.

Then someone updates your operating system and the first command's output changes. It's in a different order. Maybe the new order is prettier on the screen, but it absolutely broke that sweet command-line you spent so long creating. DAMMIT!

The reality is that most operating systems try to make sure this never happens, which is a shame. Here's what they'll do instead:

- Never change any command. Instead, make new commands, with equally obscure names, and have those do whatever new thing we want.

- Create switches that you have to use to get new output or new features. That way, the command can continue working as-is, but you can "switch" its behavior to something else. This is why the `ps` command has eleventy-dozen switches for you to remember!

Both of these are poor solutions, because they just add to the amount of information everyone has to remember.

Introducing PowerShell

First, we should get some terminology right.

In 2006, Microsoft introduced *Windows* PowerShell 1.0. Throughout the next decade, they released new versions of Windows PowerShell: 2.0, 3.0, 4.0, 5.0, and 5.1. Good times!

But for version 6, Microsoft took a different tack. In 2017, they released the first version of *PowerShell Core*, or just "PowerShell," with no "Windows" attached. It's technically version 6, but it's the first version that runs on Windows, Linux, and macOS. It's a bit trimmed-down from its Windows cousin. And, at the same time, Microsoft announced that *Windows* PowerShell would basically stop at version 5.1. Plain-old PowerShell (more properly, "PowerShell Core") is the go-forward product, and that's what this book is about.

From its beginning, though, PowerShell was designed to solve three problems, two of which are the ones I've already introduced you to.

Solution 1: Consistency

PowerShell's first step was to take all the weird command names and ditch 'em. Instead, PowerShell defines a naming pattern for its commands which is English-based, much more verbose than `grep` or `ps`, and in which the commands' names more clearly imply what the command does.

PowerShell commands consist of two parts: a verb and a noun.

The verb part comes from a fairly short, preapproved list of verbs. That way, you can start to see the consistency in the naming, and get used to it quickly. Commands that create a new thing, like a new user account or a new file, use the verb `New` (never "Create," or "Instantiate," or anything else). A command that retrieves information uses the verb `Get`. As you progress through this book, you'll meet a few of these.

The noun part is always singular, and tells you what the command is acting on. So a command that creates new users in Microsoft's Active Directory system would be `New-ADUser` (not *ADUsers*, which is plural, even if the command is actually capable of creating more than one). A command that launches an app might be called `Start-Process`. If you're not familiar with computers from a behind-the-scenes perspective, the nouns can take a little getting used to, but it's worth the effort.
A> You know, as a note, I'm always telling people that PowerShell itself is pretty easy to pick up. It's thc technologies PowerShell *touches* that get hard. Like, if you want to use PowerShell to do stuff in Microsoft's Azure cloud, it's the Azure stuff that's hard to grasp. Once you have that in your head, the PowerShell bits are easy.

Solution 2: Structured Data

PowerShell's second innovation was to ditch the textual output of commands. Oh, PowerShell can still dump a lot of text to the screen, and we'll talk about how it does that a bit later.

Instead, PowerShell commands output a kind of structured data. If you've ever seen an Excel spreadsheet, you can think of PowerShell's structured data as a bit like that. Each line of command output becomes a row in the spreadsheet. The various bits of information on each line get broken out in to the spreadsheet's columns.

The advantage of this approach is that you don't need to fuss with all the particulars of text. There's no more, "I need to find lines where the characters `httpd` show up in columns 30 through 35; instead, you just tell PowerShell "I need all the rows where the `Name` column contains `httpd`, please." It doesn't matter if the command changes in the future and the `Name` column moves from 3rd place to 6th place; PowerShell can simply track it down by using the column's name.

The structured data approach, in real-world conditions, can shave off 90% of the time spent constructing complex command lines. It's that big a deal, and as we move through this book you'll see how easy it is to work with.

Solution 3: Admin-Friendly

There's another problem that isn't specific to traditional CLIs. See, the fact is that Windows, Linux, and other operating systems already have all the tools you need to perform almost any task you might need. But most of those "tools" are really designed for software developers, and they're built in a way that is comfortable and familiar to software developers, but often confusing and antagonistic to anyone else. For example, Windows has the ability to terminate a running app. All you have to do is run code like this:

```
System.Diagonstics.Process p =
 New System.Diagnostics.Process()

 p.GetProcessById(1234)
 // assumes you know that 1234 is the app you want

p.Kill()
```

Easy, right? Well, if you're a developer, it's very easy. All you do is type in that code, compile the code into an executable, and run the executable. Takes maybe 10 minutes.

PowerShell would just want you to do this:

```
Stop-Process MyApp
```

Internally, it's that same code running! See, PowerShell *isn't actually a new tool.* It doesn't have *new capabilities.* All PowerShell does is take the capabilities the operating system already has, and "wrap them up" into an easier-to-use package that you can just type and run, right from PowerShell's CLI app. So PowerShell is potentially as powerful as your entire computer and every piece of software running on it, because PowerShell can turn almost any functionality into a more consistent, structured-data, command.

This is why PowerShell - which, remember, started in the world of Windows - has so much applicability in the worlds of Mac and Linux, as well. PowerShell isn't trying to "subvert" their native functionality, and it's not trying to make anyone learn an all-new set of tools that work differently. PowerShell is just like a "translation layer." The same `Start-Process` command can be used on Linux, Mac, or Windows; *internally*, it'll do slightly different stuff on each of those operating systems in order to make the command actually happen. But it handles all of that inside itself; as a user of PowerShell, you just need to know the one, easy-to-remember, English-like command name.

OK - Why Should I Care?

Do you know how an economy grows? Like, the economy of a country?

It works a bit like this: suppose you manufacture widgets. You have a machine that does it, and it costs about $1 per widget to make them. Your machine can make about 1,000 a day.

You decide to buy a second machine. Same kind - about 1,000 a day, and about $1 apiece. Have you grown the economy? *No.* You're producing more, but that's because you're putting more into the system, too: the machine itself, plus whatever raw materials widgets are made of.

Now suppose you decide to replace both machines with a newer, better one. This one can make 4,000 widgets a day, and they now cost $.90 to make, but you can sell them for the same price. *You have grown the economy.* For the same given input in raw materials and capital investment, you're producing more, for less. That's how economies grow.

Businesses are almost genetically programmed to grow in this way - produce more, for less. You can't just do this by keeping a close eye on paperclips, though. Reducing your costs by a small fraction isn't growing the economy, it's reducing your costs a bit. True economic growth usually requires *automation.* Ah, you perhaps see where this is going.

You see, managing servers is no different than any other kind of work that companies might do. If a company spends $x managing a server, then it can only grow its economy by spending less to manage *even more* servers. If you're managing servers by clicking around in a GUI, as we've already noted, you're never going to achieve the level of efficiency needed to grow the economy. And that's where automation comes in. If you can automate server management, then fewer inputs (administrator people) can produce more output (manage more servers), and that's economic growth.

PowerShell isn't the only way to automate server administration. But, as we pointed out in this chapter, PowerShell solves many of the problems that other techniques have introduced, so it's arguably *more efficient* than other, older automation techniques. *More efficient* means a bigger boost to the economy, and PowerShell's often easier to learn, to boot.

Let's assume you work in the server management business, and that you're paid $50,000 a year (a nice round number, because I'm terrible at math). Your "fully loaded" salary - including benefits, payroll taxes, and so on - is about 40% higher, or about $70,000 (this is in the US; outside the US, the number is probably quite different, and you'd need to ask an HR specialist for your particular country's fully loaded salary multiplier). Divide that by 2,000, which is about the number of working hours in a year, for an hourly rate of $35.

Now suppose you have a task that you have to complete all the time, and it takes ten minutes. Therefore, that costs your employer about $5.83 every time you do it. If you spent an hour setting PowerShell up to perform that task, it'd cost you a one-time charge of $35, and then the task would essentially *cost nothing* to perform in the future. After PowerShell performed the task just *six times*, you'd have paid off your investment, and every time PowerShell performed the task after that, *you'd be growing the economy.* Work would be happening, essentially for free. That's how Henry Ford did it, and that's why you should care about PowerShell. The first line on your resume should be, "Dedicated automation specialist who, in one year, saved former employer $100k [or whatever] in labor costs."

Keep a log of what you automate. Figure out how long the task took to perform manually, and about how many times a year it was performed. Track the time it took you to automate it. Figure out the money you saved, and add that to your resume statement.

That is why you should care about PowerShell.

4. Installing PowerShell

So, this is where we need to make sure we're all *very on board* with terminology.

Windows PowerShell

Windows PowerShell runs on the full .NET Framework, and runs only on Windows. As of this writing, it's version 5.1, although that version will not run on very old versions of Windows. Windows PowerShell is supported as part of the operating system it is installed on, which means Microsoft's standard OS support policies apply. Windows PowerShell is installed as part of a package called Windows Management Framework (WMF), and you can download that from http://microsoft.com/powershell. *Most* versions of Windows do some with Windows PowerShell preinstalled, although it might not be the latest version. Within PowerShell, you can run:

```
PS C:\> $PSVersionTable
```

And you can see the version of Windows PowerShell, .NET Framework, and other components. If you aren't on the latest version, Windows Update may offer a newer version as an optional update, or you can download it from http://microsoft.com/powershell.

It's probably best to read and follow the instructions at https://docs.microsoft.com/en-us/powershell/scripting/setup/installing-windows-powershell?view=powershell-6, which also detail version compatibility.

Windows PowerShell 5.1 is not supported on any version of Windows prior to Windows 7 SP1 or Windows Server 2008 R2 SP1.

PowerShell Core

PowerShell Core is a *different piece of software* than Windows PowerShell. On Windows systems, you can have both Windows PowerShell *and* PowerShell Core installed, and can even run them side by side. Running this:

```
PS C:\> $PSVersionTable
```

Will tell you which one you're currently using, and it's important to keep track. Add-ins and scripts written for Windows PowerShell won't always work in PowerShell Core, so you need to carefully differentiate between them on Windows systems.

The online docs[1] cover installation instructions for Windows, various Linux distributions, and macOS. **Read the installation instructions very carefully** because there are often prerequisites you need to install first. That URL defaults to the Windows installation instructions; links (on the left side, as of this writing) to the macOS and Linux versions are provided.

In most cases you will need administrator or super-user access in order to install PowerShell.

[1]https://docs.microsoft.com/en-us/powershell/scripting/setup/installing-powershell-core-on-windows?view=powershell-6

VS Code

Windows PowerShell ships with a simple editor called the Integrated Scripting Environment, or "PowerShell ISE." This is technically a deprecated editor; while it still works, Microsoft isn't developing it any further. Instead, Microsoft suggests you use Visual Studio Code, which is a stripped-down, cross-platform, free editor that can be extended to accommodate different languages.

Head to https://code.visualstudio.com to download VS Code for your operating system. You'll then want to install the PowerShell Extensions for VS Code, so that VS Code "understands" PowerShell's language. Instructions for Windows, macOS, and Linux are available online.[2] But basically, once you've got VS Code installed, open it and press Ctrl+P or Cmd+P. Type `ext install powershell`, hit Return, and you'll see the PowerShell extension. Click its little **Install** button, and allow VS Code to **Reload** after installation finishes.

When you start in VS Code, you'll want to open a new file using the File menu, and then immediately save it using one of PowerShell's filename extensions. For example, a filename like `Myscript.ps1` or anything else with a `.ps1` filename extension. Saving the file like that is what "tells" VS Code that this is a PowerShell file, and so it will engage the PowerShell Extension and start working correctly for the PowerShell syntax.

---

[2]https://docs.microsoft.com/en-us/powershell/scripting/core-powershell/vscode/using-vscode?view=powershell-6

Don't feel you need to install VS Code right away. Most of this book will have you working in PowerShell's command-line console, not in VS Code or in the ISE. Both VS Code and the ISE work a little differently than the console when it comes to running commands, so we truly recommend you just stick with the normal console app as you get started, and switch to VS Code when you're ready to start scripting.

5. Your First Console Experience

This is a great place to start following along. If you've not already installed PowerShell, go ahead and do that (from the previous chapter), and then jump in.

Launch PowerShell

On Windows systems, you can press Windows+R to get the Run dialog, and then type `powershell` and hit Return to open the shell. We find it convenient to pin its icon to the Task bar once it's running. On systems with both Windows PowerShell and PowerShell Core, you may need to dig through the Start menu to find the one you want to run.

A big note on Windows systems: Normally, PowerShell will launch as a low-privileged user account, not as Administrator. However, most of the time, you'll be performing tasks that require Administrator permissions. The Windows PowerShell window title bar will say `Administrator` if you're running with elevated privileges. If you're not, and you need to, right-click the Task bar icon and select "Run as Administrator." This will open a new window, which should say `Administrator` in the title bar.

On macOS and Linux systems, open a command prompt (that's the Terminal app on macOS, located in the Application

- Utilities folder), type `pwsh`, and press Return. A new window won't open; you'll be "in" PowerShell right in the same terminal window. PowerShell uses a module called PSReadLine that provides enhanced console capabilities like tab completion and coloring; I've found that certain command-line color schemes don't work well with PSReadLine. We often need to stick with a basic black background, for example, or things get weird, color-wise. Just be aware of that.

Having trouble? Stop now and get help. The PowerShell Q&A Forums on PowerShell.org are a good place to start. You'll need to log in (or create an account), and be aware that some browsers aggressively cache the not-logged-in page. If you log in, and then go back to a page that implies (or says) you're not logged in, force your browser to reload the page (Shift and the Reload button, for example) from the server. You can also try pinging me @concentratedDon on Twitter, although understand that answering technical questions in 250 characters or so can be pretty challenging.

Check Your Version

Next, let's check the version of PowerShell to make sure you're running what you expected. At the prompt, type `$PSVersionTable` and hit Return. You should get some output detailing the version, like 5.1 or 6.0, and the edition, like Windows or Core.

If you don't get that output, **stop**. Something's wrong. You're probably not running PowerShell, after all. Go back and double-check your work, ask for help if you need it, and make sure `$PSVersionTable` is working before you continue.

Run a Command

Type `Get-Process` and hit Return. You should get a big 'ol screen full of output, showing all of the apps (including background ones that you may never have even been aware of) running on your computer right then.

This is a good time to talk about PowerShell *aliases*. These are just nicknames for commands. Like, if you find `Get-Process` too hard to type, then you could just type its alias, `ps`. Except for one problem. You see, when *Windows* PowerShell launched, the product team thought it would be a good idea to include Unix-like aliases for PowerShell commands. So in PowerShell, you'd run `Get-Process`, but on Linux systems the closest equivalent is `ps`. Since Windows PowerShell didn't run on Linux, this wasn't a problem. If you were really familiar with Linux, and you just habitually typed `ps`, then PowerShell would do something that was roughly what you were thinking of.

When PowerShell Core was introduced, though, this created a conundrum, because `ps` is a legitimate command on some of the operating systems where PowerShell Core runs, like Linux and macOS. If a Linux person sits down at a Linux machine and types `ps`, but gets the output of `Get-Process` instead, that Linux person is going to be a little irritated. So PowerShell Core doesn't define the `ps` alias on Linux; if you run `ps`, you're getting the really-for-real `ps` from Linux, not the PowerShell `Get-Process` command.

Yeah, this gets confusing. As a result, I'm just not going to use any aliases with you. I'm not saying aliases are good or bad, just that they're not consistent across systems, and we don't want to have to keep differentiating between Windows and Linux and macOS. So I'll just use the full PowerShell command names, which, thanks to their *verb-noun* naming pattern, are pretty easy to distinguish.

But PowerShell command names can be *long*, and gosh, typing is just so hard, isn't it? That's why aliases were created in part, right? Because they're shorter! So rather than subject you to a lifetime of typing long command names, let me introduce you to Tab completion. The Tab key, on most keyboards, is an oversized key toward the upper-left side of the keyboard. The Tab key is bigger because you're *meant to use it.* It's easier to hit with your finger, so it's a convenient way to make typing shorter.

In PowerShell again, type `Get-P`, and then hit Tab. PowerShell will start "filling in" command names that match whatever you typed up to that point. Keep hitting `Tab` until `Get-Process` shows up, and hit Return. With some practice, you start to quickly figure out how much you have to type to get what you need with just one Tab or two.

At this point, you've run your first PowerShell command! It might not feel like it, but you're well on your way to mastering this thing!

Files and Folders

Windows and Linux have different ideas about file systems, but PowerShell (well, PowerShell *Core*) understands them both. To begin, run `Get-PSDrive` in your own copy of PowerShell. On my Mac, we get something like this:

```
PS /Users/donjones> get-psdrive                                      \
Name       Used (GB)   Free (GB) Provider    Root                    \
----       ---------   --------- --------    ----                    \
/             266.04      665.51 FileSystem     /                    \
Alias                            Alias                               \
Env                              Environment                         \
Function                         Function                            \
Variable                         Variable
```

The Alias, Env, Function, and Variable drives are common to all versions of PowerShell. On my Unix-based Mac system, we also have a / drive, which is the main storage unit in the computer. Windows systems will commonly have a `C:` drive for that "system" drive, and may also have drives like `D:` for an optical disc reader (like a DVD drive). Your computer may have others.

Windows and Linux/macOS also differ in that Windows likes to use the backslash \ when it deals with files and folders, and Linux (and macOS) prefers a forward slash / character. PowerShell doesn't care. You can use either slash on any operating system without having to worry about it.

Start by changing to the "root," or top level, of your system drive. For Linux and macOS people:

```
Set-Location /
```

Windows users:

```
Set-Location C:\
```

PowerShell defines an alias, `cd`, that you can use instead of `Set-Location`. It's an alias that's the same on all operating systems, and if you prefer using it, feel free to do so. Now, get a listing of files and folders in this "root" location:

```
Get-ChildItem
```

On any operating system, you could also use the alias `dir`. Don't use `ls`, though; while it will work as expected on Windows systems, on Linux and macOS it runs the native `ls` command, which is very different. And this is the *last* time I'll bring up aliases! From now on, I'll just use full command names and rely on Tab completion to lighten the typing load.

Now, I'm going to change to my "home" folder. This is a thing PowerShell tracks in its special `$home` placeholder, so it'll work on any operating system.

```
Set-Location $home
```

Now, we want to make a new folder that we can play in, store some test files in, and so on. To do that, I'll use the `New-Item` command. This command is capable of creating many types of new items, and so in addition to the name of the new item, we'll have to tell it what *kind* of item to create. In this case, a folder, or `Directory`. You should be able to use Tab completion to complete most of this:

```
New-Item -Path 4n00bs -ItemType Directory
```

In fact, to emphasize the Tab completion, I'll show you where we pressed Tab by inserting a *. You can't type this as-is; but if you press Tab wherever you see a *, you should get the correct result:

```
New-It* -P* 4n00bs -It* D*
```

Make sure the final command reads the same as the one above. You won't be able to run the command twice, so if you've already done so and you hit Return on the second one, you'll get an error, telling you that the 4n00bs directory already exists:

```
New-Item : An item with the specified name
/Users/donjones/4n00bs already exists.
At line:1 char:1
+ New-Item -Path 4n00bs -ItemType Directory
+ ~~~~~~~~~~~~~~~~~~~~~~~~~~~~~~~~~~~~~~~~~
    + CategoryInfo          : ResourceExists: (/Use\
rs/donjones/
   4n00bs:String) [New-Item], IOException
    + FullyQualifiedErrorId : DirectoryExist,Micros\
oft.PowerShe
   ll.Commands.NewItemCommand
```

Don't let errors panic you too much. Yeah, they're red, and they do remind me of every bad English paper we turned in in high school, but they contain useful information most of the time. This one is telling us that `4n00bs` already exists. It's showing us the PowerShell command it had a problem with, and it's showing some of the underlying "technical" information about the error record itself. Error messages can be a great way of diagnosing problems, if you're patient enough to really read them, instead of just panicking, slamming the lid of your laptop closed, and going home for the day.

Exit

To exit, either type `exit` and hit Return, or just close the command-line window.

A Good First Step

This was a decent first step, and it was just intended to kind of acclimate you to PowerShell. You've launched the shell, run a few commands, and even created a fresh folder for future use. Before we go any further, it's time to dig a little deeper into these commands we're running.

6. Where Do Commands Come From?

This is probably one of the most important topics we'll get to in PowerShell, so while this chapter is a bit long, every word is worth it, we promise.

So. `Get-ChildItem`. `Set-Location`. `New-Item`. `Get-Process`. Those are the commands you learned in the previous chapter, and there are only 22,384 left to go. Kidding! There are probably *way* more than that. So we need to discuss first where commands actually come from.

You see, when a mommy command and a daddy command love each other *very much*, they...

Mmmm, no. Let's do this differently. First, you need to know that PowerShell commands come packaged in something called a *module*. A module can have one or more commands, help files, and lots of other stuff. So, where do modules come from?

Built-In Commands

This is one of the first confusing things newcomers run into with PowerShell, especially Windows PowerShell. There are really two distinct categories of *built-in*, and it's crucial that you understand the difference.

First, there are the **commands built into PowerShell itself**. Windows PowerShell came with a lot more than PowerShell Core, which tends to rely on external sources of commands. Each new version of PowerShell came with more commands than the last one, and any computer running that version of PowerShell would have all of that version's commands (as you might expect).

But then there are the **commands built into the Windows operating system**. You use this *in* PowerShell, but they don't *come with* PowerShell. Take Windows 7 as an example. It came with Windows PowerShell v2, and only a couple of small modules of its own. So you couldn't do a ton with it. Windows 8 shipped not long after, and came with *tons* of commands, as well as Windows PowerShell v3. So Windows 7 owners excitedly installed Windows PowerShell v3 on their Windows 7 systems... and were disappointed, because they didn't get very many new commands. *Most* of the awesome new stuff in Windows 8 *was part of Windows 8 itself*, not part of the Windows PowerShell v3 product. So the version of Windows you're on would largely determine what commands you had, regardless of the version of Windows PowerShell you had.

And *then* there are the modules that come with a particular *type* of operating system, like Windows Server. Windows Server comes with modules for managing all of the server software it can run, like DNS Server or Active Directory, but those modules don't come with the client versions of Windows. However, Microsoft does make most of them available in their Remote Server Administration Toolkit, or RSAT. Install the RSAT on your version of Windows, and you'll get all those "server commands." Which leads nicely into the second main place commands come from...

Comes with Software

Many software applications come with PowerShell modules designed to help manage that particular application. Microsoft SQL Server does, Microsoft SharePoint Server does, and so on. Other times, vendors make their modules available as a separate download. VMware does that with their PowerCLI package, for example, which helps manage their vSphere product. Each vendor is a bit different so you'll have to check with them to see if they offer PowerShell support, and how you get it.

> Remember, modules written for Windows PowerShell won't always work in PowerShell Core. That's because those modules depend on pieces of the Windows operating system in addition to PowerShell itself, and since those pieces aren't on other operating systems, PowerShell Core can't support them even if it happens to be running on Windows. You'll have to check on each module that you want to use, and contact its vendor or author, to determine compatibility.

The Internet

Of course, you can always just download stuff from the Internet. Search Google and cross your fingers! Some modules distributed on the Internet may come with an installer you have to run, while others may just require you to copy some files to a specific location. These days, though, the Internet method of module distribution is being replaced by...

PowerShell Gallery

PowerShellGallery.com is a Microsoft-run *repository* of PowerShell scripts, modules, and other kinds of resources. It's where the cool kids share their PowerShell modules these days, and it's the main source we'll be focusing on here.

You can start by simply visiting the web site and searching or browsing through the available modules. *There are a lot.* But at some point you're going to want to download some of them to your computer, to start using them in PowerShell.

> Neither Microsoft nor we make any kind of promise or warranty about the modules in PowerShell Gallery. Literally anyone can upload anything, with no quality checks of any kind. So you should investigate modules before you use them. Are people talking about the module on other web sites (a Google search can help you check)? Is the author someone you've heard of, with a good reputation? Modules run the gamut from "amazing" to "poorly written" and I'm sure, in some cases, "outright malicious," so use caution.

PowerShell interacts directly with PowerShell Gallery through a module called *PowerShellGet*, which in turn is built on Microsoft's *PackageManagement* module. It's built into PowerShell Core and in Windows PowerShell v5 and later; for earlier versions of Windows PowerShell, the PowerShell-Gallery.com website has download packages so that you can install PowerShellGet.

We've decided that we want to play around with making some HTML-formatted reports in PowerShell, and we want to see if there are any modules that can help.

```
Find-Module \*html\*

Version    Name                      Repository  \

-------    ----                      ----------  \

1.0.0.98   ConvertToHtml             PSGallery   \

2.1.0.1    EnhancedHTML2             PSGallery   \

1.0.1      Write-HtmlNode            PSGallery   \

0.1.1      HtmlReport                PSGallery   \

1.4.0.3    ReportHTML                PSGallery   \

0.0.1      pshtmltable               PSGallery   \

0.0.0.2    ReportHTMLHelpers         PSGallery   \

1.2.6      MarkdownToHtml            PSGallery   \

0.1.6      PowerHTML                 PSGallery
```

> The first time Windows PowerShell users try this, you may be prompted to install stuff like NuGet, and prompted to trust the PowerShell Gallery repository. You'll need to agree to these tasks in order for PowerShellGet to work.

We searched for `\*html\*` because the * character represents a *wildcard*. That is, it can "stand in" for any one or more other characters. As you can see, it's returned a handful of items containing "html" in their name. I'm going to install "EnhancedHTML2," because it was written by an upstanding guy (Don) and we trust him (Don).

```
Install-Module EnhancedHTML2


Untrusted repository
You are installing the modules from an untrusted re\
pository. If
you trust this repository, change its InstallationP\
olicy value by
 running the Set-PSRepository cmdlet. Are you sure \
you want to
install the modules from 'PSGallery'?
[Y] Yes  [A] Yes to All  [N] No  [L] No to All  [S]\
 Suspend
[?] Help(default is "N"): y
```

As you can see, we were prompted because PSGallery (PowerShell Gallery's internal nickname) is *untrusted*. We tend to leave it set to untrusted, because it's got a lot of stuff from people we don't know. That way, we're prompted each time we install something, and we can stop and have a nice, sober thinking moment before we do anything else. In this case, we've responded with a "y," indicating that we want to proceed. The module installs, and we're good to go. If it hadn't installed, there would be error messages alerting me to the problem.

We'll have a look at the installed module in just a second.

PowerShellGet can also update modules, if a new version becomes available; just run `Update-Module`. Or, if you want to see the gritty details of what it's doing, run `Update-Module -Verbose`. And it can also remove modules you no longer need, by using `Remove-Module`. Note that it can only remove modules that it installed; modules that came from elsewhere can't be removed that way.

Your Own Gallery

PowerShell Gallery is based on a repository technology called *NuGet* (pronounced, "nougat," like the candy). Many companies set up their own private Nuget repositories, which you can access the same way that you'd access PowerShell Gallery. If you work in one of these organizations, ask your IT colleagues how to register and use their private PowerShell module repository.

Seeing What Modules and Commands You Have

So - how can you quickly see what modules you've got installed?

```
Get-Module -ListAvailable

    Directory:
    /usr/local/microsoft/powershell/6.0.0-beta.3/Mo\
dules


ModuleType Version Name
---------- ------- ----
Script     2.1.0.1 EnhancedHTML2
Manifest   1.1.0.0 Microsoft.PowerShell.Archive
Manifest   3.0.0.0 Microsoft.PowerShell.Host
Manifest   3.1.0.0 Microsoft.PowerShell.Management \
Manifest   3.0.0.0 Microsoft.PowerShell.Security
Manifest   3.1.0.0 Microsoft.PowerShell.Utility
Script     1.1.4.0 PackageManagement
Script     3.3.9   Pester
Script     1.1.3.1 PowerShellGet
Script     0.0     PSDesiredStateConfiguration
Script     1.2     PSReadLine
```

You can see that we don't have many, which is because we ran this in a fairly basic PowerShell Core installation on macOS. A Windows computer would list many more modules, in most cases, especially in Windows PowerShell (versus PowerShell Core). Of especial note is the directory shown near the top of the output: this tells you where PowerShell is "looking" for modules. You can (and should) also run this:

```
$env:PSModulePath
/Users/donjones/.local/share/powershell/Modules:/us\
r/local/share/powershell/Modules:/usr/local/microso\
ft/powershell/6.0.0-beta.3/Modules
```

This is the complete list of where PowerShell keeps its modules. So long as a module is contained in one of these locations, PowerShell can "find" it and use it automatically.

What's in a Module?

Modules consist, for the most part, of *commands*. There are actually several kinds of things in PowerShell that are all considered *commands*, and since they basically all work the same, you don't need to worry much (at this stage) what the differences are. Try this (assuming you've been following along to this point):

```
Get-Command -Module EnhancedHTML2

CommandType     Name                                  \

-----------     ----                                  \

Function        ConvertTo-EnhancedHTML
Function        ConvertTo-EnhancedHTMLFragment
```

So this module contains two commands, both of which are of the *function* sub-type, and you can see the command names right there, clear as day. You can do this with any installed module, although some of them contain a *lot* of commands, so just be prepared for that to scroll by on the screen!

> There's a situation on the Windows operating system, in both Windows PowerShell and PowerShell Core, that you need to be aware of. This can especially crop up when you try to run a command that's been installed from the Internet, like we just did with **EnhancedHTML2**. That situation is called the *execution policy.*
>
> On Windows, the execution policy decides what scripts (and many modules are just a kind of script) can run. It defaults to **Restricted**, which basically means, "no scripts." So you'll need to modify that, and you'll need to be running PowerShell "as Administrator" to do so.
>
> Set-ExecutionPolicy Unrestricted
>
> Two caveats: first, we're totally not explaining what this is doing for right now, although you should definitely take the time to learn more in the next chapter. Second, if you're on a company-owned computer, your company may limit your ability to change this setting, and PowerShell will display a warning if that's the case.

Explore What's Out There

Spend some time exploring PowerShell Gallery and seeing what's there. Honestly, two-thirds of the "battle" in PowerShell is finding the commands that will do whatever it is you need to do, and browsing the Gallery can start to give you an idea of what's out there, and what's possible.

7. How Do I Use This Thing?

OK, so let's say that you've wrapped your head around the idea of searching for modules than can do what you need, and you know how to get a list of commands within a module. How do you run those commands?

Windows Only: ExecutionPolicy

This is a bit of a big, hotly debated topic that we're going to gloss over pretty heavily. *Learn Windows PowerShell in a Month of Lunches* covers this in a lot more detail, and our goal here is just to get you up and running quickly.

ExecutionPolicy, on Windows, is designed to limit the ability for someone to accidentally execute an untrusted script. We want you to notice how many little weasel words we used there:

- Limit (not prevent)
- Accidentally (not deliberately)
- Untrusted (not any)

Know that *anyone* can launch a copy of Windows PowerShell *and change the execution policy to whatever they want at that time*, and their selection will "last" for the duration of that PowerShell session. So this isn't designed to stop a determined, knowledgable person from doing anything.

Also know that *you can't do anything in PowerShell that you can't do in ten other ways.* You can't use PowerShell to delete a file that you wouldn't already be able to delete in Windows in some other way, for example. PowerShell isn't a security gate; it's just another way to do things that you're already allowed to do.

ExecutionPolicy isn't meant to ward off malware (you should have anti-malware applications for that) or to stop attackers (they've dozens of other ways to do what they need to do).

Because we're trying to get *you* to be a knowledgeable, deliberate user of PowerShell, in the previous chapter we asked you to set your ExecutionPolicy to **Unrestricted**:

```
Set-ExecutionPolicy Unrestricted
```

This will let you follow along with the examples in this book, and so long as you're *careful* and *deliberate* (meaning, not hasty), then you'll be fine. You won't be "opening up" any "security holes," either.

It's Okay to Ask for Help

PowerShell has a deep and actually useful help system, and this chapter is all about using it. We're being honest with you when we say that, if you really master the help system, you'll easily master the shell.

Update Help

Your first step, and a step you should repeat every couple of months, is to update the local help files stored on your computer.

```
Update-Help
```

Now, there are two things that may go wrong here. Here's the first one:

```
update-help : Failed to update Help for the module(\
s) 'Microsoft.PowerShell.Archive, Microsoft.PowerSh\
ell.Core, Microsoft.PowerShell.Host, Microsoft.Powe\
rShell.Management, Microsoft.PowerShell.Security, M\
icrosoft.PowerShell.Utility, PackageManagement, Pow\
erShellGet, PSReadLine' with UI culture(s) {en-US} \
: Access to the path '/usr/local/microsoft/powershe\
ll/6.0.2/en-US/Microsoft.PowerShell.Commands.Utilit\
y.dll-Help.xml' is denied.
At line:1 char:1
+ update-help
+ ~~~~~~~~~~~
+ CategoryInfo          : InvalidOperation: (:) [Up\
date-Help], Exception
+ FullyQualifiedErrorId : UnknownErrorId,Microsoft.\
PowerShell.Commands.UpdateHelpCommand
```

Ouch. Here's the reason:

```
Access to the path '/usr/local/microsoft/powershell\
/6.0.2/en-US/Microsoft.PowerShell.Commands.Utility.\
dll-Help.xml' is denied.
```

You didn't have permission to update the old version of the file, most often because it's stored in a protected folder. This is *really* common on Windows systems because all of the built-in commands' help is in Windows' System32 folder, which mere mortals aren't allowed to access. The solution? Run the shell as Administrator, as we've outlined previously. Or, on Linux or macOS, run PowerShell as administrator using the `sudo` command.

The other thing that can, and often does, go wrong is that help won't be found online. This is normal and expected. Many modules simply don't publish online help updates, and that's especially true of non-Microsoft modules. So you should always read the error message carefully and decide if it's actually a problem or not.

Finding Commands and Help

Once you've got most of your local help updated, there are two tasks you'll need to perform. One is finding commands, and the other is finding help files for them. They might seem like the same thing, but while they're definitely related, they're different.

Finding commands lets you see what you've got installed locally *whether someone wrote a help file for the command or not.* On the other hand *finding help* lets you find *help files,* even if they're not related to a command. So you see, they're both useful tasks, and they're the first step toward figuring out how to use PowerShell.

```
PS /> get-command *proc*

CommandType     Name
-----------     ----
Function        Get-PSMetaConfigurationProcessed
Function        Set-PSMetaConfigDocInsProcessedBefo\
reMeta
Cmdlet          Debug-Process
Cmdlet          Get-Process
Cmdlet          Start-Process
Cmdlet          Stop-Process
Cmdlet          Wait-Process
Application     creatbyproc.d
Application     filebyproc.d
Application     fixproc
Application     newproc.d
Application     procsystime
Application     sampleproc
Application     syscallbyproc.d
Application     topsysproc
Application     xsltproc
```

Here, we used `Get-Command` and gave it a *wildcard pattern*, in which * represents "any zero or more characters." As you can see, the command returned a list of all commands on our system containing the characters "proc," and the list includes PowerShell functions, cmdlets (pronounced *command-lets*, these are written in a .NET language like C#), and applications, which are anything external to PowerShell itself.

We normally tend to use a bit more of a nuanced command search, because PowerShell's "verb-noun" naming syntax makes it easier to narrow things down more rapidly.

```
PS /> get-command -verb get -noun *proc*

CommandType     Name
-----------     ----
Function        Get-PSMetaConfigurationProcessed
Cmdlet          Get-Process
```

This is a much shorter list to deal with. Once we know the command we want, we can ask for help. But we could also have done this "search" using the help system:

```
PS /> get-help *proc*

Name                              Category  Module
----                              --------  ------
Debug-Process                     Cmdlet    Micr...
Get-Process                       Cmdlet    Mic...
Start-Process                     Cmdlet    Mic...
Stop-Process                      Cmdlet    Mic...
Wait-Process                      Cmdlet    Mic...
Get-PSMetaConfigurationProcessed  Function  PSD...
Set-PSMetaConfigDocInsProcesse... Function  PSD...
```

You can see that this is a slightly different list, because it's looking for help files, not commands. There are no help files for the built-in applications on the computer, because those are external to PowerShell, and so they don't show up on this list. Here's another time you'll see the difference between help and commands:

```
Get-Help about*
```

Try that yourself, because on Windows in particular it'll return a big, long list. These *about* files are PowerShell's user manual.

Once you've got the help file you want, just ask for help on it:

```
Get-Help Get-Process -Full
```

We almost always ask for that `-Full` help, because it's got *so* much more in it.

You can add `-ShowWindow` in Windows PowerShell to get your local help in a floating window; this doesn't work in PowerShell Core. Also, you can use the alias `help` instead of the full `Get-Help` command name in any version of PowerShell.

Online Help

It's also never a bad idea to punch your favorite command name into Google or Bing, since the top results will likely be the web-based version of the help file. That's especially nice if you're working on a system where you don't have permission to update help, or if you want the help to appear in a separate window (making it easy to refer to while you continue to work in PowerShell).

Reading the Help Files

Let's start with the basic stuff at the top of the help file:

```
NAME
    Get-Process

SYNTAX
    Get-Process [[-Name] <string[]>] [-Module] [-Fi\
leVersionInfo]  [<CommonParameters>]

    Get-Process [[-Name] <string[]>] -IncludeUserNa\
me  [<CommonParameters>]

    Get-Process -Id <int[]> [-Module] [-FileVersion\
Info]  [<CommonParameters>]

    Get-Process -Id <int[]> -IncludeUserName  [<Com\
monParameters>]

    Get-Process -InputObject <Process[]> -IncludeUs\
erName  [<CommonParameters>]

    Get-Process -InputObject <Process[]> [-Module] \
[-FileVersionInfo]  [<CommonParameters>]
```

This is the *syntax section* and it provides a basic rundown on how to use the command. You'll notice in this case that it contains six different variations, or *parameter sets*. A parameter set is just a different way of running the command. For example, sometimes at the grocery store you might go to the limited-items express lane, other times the full-service lane, and other times a self-service lane. Those are all like different parameter sets; they all get the job done, and you end up with the same outcome, but you operate each one a little differently.

Each parameter set is differentiated by its combination of

parameters. This is a bit like those magazine puzzles, where you're shown an altered photo and the unaltered original, and you have to spot the seven or so differences between them. In the case of parameter sets, you have to spot the parameter or parameters that exit only in each set.

1. The first one has -Name, but not -IncludeUserName
2. The second one has -Name and -IncludeUserName
3. The third has -Id, but not -IncludeUserName
4. The fourth has -Id and -IncludeUserName
5. The fifth has -InputObject, and -IncludeUserName
6. The sixth has -InputObject, but not -IncludeUserName

So each of these can be distinguished by either `-Name`, `-ID`, or `-InputObject`, and whether or not `-IncludeUserName` was used. And we've no idea why 5 and 6 broke the pattern.

Let's drill into just one of these:

```
Get-Process [[-Name] <string[]>] [-Module] [-FileVe\
rsionInfo]  [<CommonParameters>]
```

Some parameters accept an input value, like `-Name` does. The <angle brackets> tell you the data type, which in this case is a String, meaning text that contains letters, numbers, and possibly symbols. Jason calls these *chahooahooas.* The [] square brackets, when they're right up against each other, means that the parameter can accept more than one value, which you'd ordinarily separate with commas: `-Name One,Two,Three`. Jason calls these brackets *binkies.*

Notice that the *entire* `-Name` parameter, including its string value, is in [square brackets]? That means the entire parameter is optional - you don't need to use it. In fact, *every* parameter in this parameter set is option, which means you could just run `Get-Process` by itself. Try it.

But the actual `-Name` portion is also in a separate set of [binkies], which means *you don't have to type the parameter name!* You could just run `Get-Process p*`. PowerShell guesses that you wanted `p*` fed to the `-Name` parameter based on its *position*. Positional parameters can save you a bit of typing, but they can really mess you up, because if you start stringing a bunch of them together and get the order wrong, the command won't run correctly. Positional parameters also make it harder to read the command in the future, because you have to go look up which parameter each value is connecting to. So we recommend using parameter names most of the time, rather than relying on positional parameters.

What about parameters like `-Module` or `-FileVersionInfo`? They don't have a value type listed, which makes them *switches*. They're either on, or off, like a light switch. Most will default to "off," meaning if you don't include the parameter, then whatever it does will not happen. So if you want module information or file version info included in this command's output, you have to specify `-Module` or `-FileVersionInfo` to "switch on" those features.

Finally, what're those "common parameters?" They're a set of "universal" parameters that PowerShell itself adds to every function or cmdlet. Hey, here's a chance to practice your help skills: try using Google or Bing to search for "about_common-parameters" and see what comes up!

If you're looking at the full help (which would include any online help files), then you'll also find per-parameter breakdowns like this:

```
    -FileVersionInfo

        Required?                    false
        Position?                    Named
        Accept pipeline input?       false
        Parameter set name           Id, InputObjec\
t, Name
        Aliases                      FV, FVI
        Dynamic?                     false
```

This reinforces what the brackets all spelled out in the more concise syntax section. This parameter isn't required, and it can't be used positionally - you have to actually write out the parameter name. It's a member of three parameter sets.

There's a trick with parameter names you should know about. Well, two tricks, really. First, you only ever need to type enough of the parameter name to distinguish from other parameters. So typing `-FileV` would be just as good as the full `-FileVersionInfo`. Of course, thanks to the magic of tab completion, if you typed `-FileV` you might as well tap the Tab key and finish the parameter name. Doing so makes it easier to read! The second trick is that some parameters have *aliases*, or nicknames. In this case, we can see that `-FV` would be just as good as -FileVersionInfo, in terms of typing. Of course, in terms of *reading*, `-FV` isn't as descriptive, so we still tend to recommend using the full parameter name.

Finally, most help files will include a number of helpful examples, which show you how to use the command. We can't stress enough how useful and important these are! About 90% of the time, when we're answering questions in the PowerShell.org forums, the answer was right in the help file examples all along!

8. Objects and the Magic of Formatting

One thing that can be a little abstract about PowerShell is this notion of *objects*, the structured data that most PowerShell commands output. The reason it's a little abstract is that you can't easily *see* the darn things. Here's why: when you run a PowerShell command, like this:

```
Get-Process
```

PowerShell is secretly tacking something on to the end. In reality, you're running this:

```
Get-Process | Out-Default
```

The `Out-Default` command is internally hardwired to redirect objects to `Out-Host`. That command, like many of the `Out-` commands, invokes PowerShell's *formatting system*, whose job it is to take all of those "structured data objects" and turn them into something a human being can read and deal with. So when you run `Get-Process` and you get a pretty table of data (go on, try it), it's because a lot of magic was happening behind the scenes to create that text display you're seeing. It's easy to assume that the text display *is the output of the command*, but nothing could be further from the truth. The whole reason PowerShell exists, in fact, is that *there is no text* until every command on the line has finished running.

PowerShell then takes whatever is in the pipeline and tries to create a sensible, human-readable text display from it. For example, if you ran this:

```
Get-Process | Where Name -like 's*'
```

The `Get-Process` command is producing those structured objects, and *piping* them to the `Where` command (in reality, the command is `Where-Object`; many of the `-Object` commands have a convenient alias that simply omits the `-Object` part of the name to make the whole command read more like an English sentence). There `Where` command doesn't have to figure out "which column of text contains the name," because it isn't dealing with text. It simply looks up the Name "column" in the structured data, and keeps the "rows" where that value starts with the letter `s`. Whatever comes out of the `Where` command secretly goes to `Out-Default`, which invokes `Out-Host`, which runs the formatting system to produce a text display of whatever was produced.

In PowerShell, nothing becomes text until the end of the pipeline. Until then, it's structured data.

The above is such an important statement! It's also the root cause behind most of PowerShell's "gotchas" that trip up newcomers. The output you see on the screen, after running a command, isn't necessarily the actual data that the command generated. The formatting system can "massage" the data to create an attractive-looking display, but it can mislead you about what you actually have to work with. The formatting system can rename columns, reformat the data (turning bytes into megabytes, for example), add carriage returns, and more.

Formatting Rules

So what does this magic, unseen formatting system actually decide to do with your objects? There's actually a simple rule set.

First, the system looks to see *what type of structured data* it's dealing with. In .NET Framework, which is what PowerShell is built on, every possible type of structured data has a unique name, appropriately called a *type name*. The objects output by `Get-Process` have the *type name* `System.Diagnostics.Process`. You an see this by running:

```
Get-Process | Get-Member
```

The `Get-Member` command is designed to show you the details about the data structured piped to it, rather than the contents of those structures as you're used to.

Go on, try it â€” run the above command and see what you get. See where it says the type name?

Once the formatting system knows the type name, it can run through its rules.

1. Often times, Microsoft or another developer will have created a set of instructions called a *formatting view*, that tell the formatting system how to turn the objects' data into a text display. These instructions live in XML-based files on disk, and some of them are installed along with PowerShell itself. This is where the formatting system can do the most work in terms of "massaging" your data.

2. If there isn't a formatting view for the type in question, PowerShell looks to see how many properties, or "columns," the structured data has. If the number is 5 or less, the formatting system constructs a text table. If it's 6 or more, the system creates a list.

That's it! There's only those two rules. Of course, you can override that behavior anytime you want to. You do this by intercepting the objects before they make it to the secret `Out-Default` command. For example, to force PowerShell to make a list:

```
Get-Process | Format-List
```

It's crucial to understand that `Format-` commands *consume* whatever you pipe into them, and produce a special kind of data that's designed to create a text display. In other words, after `Format-List` runs, our `System.Diagnostics.Process` objects are gone, and in their place is basically a bunch of proprietary structures that PowerShell uses to display text. **Once you've engaged a `Format-` command, you really can't do anything else with the data.**

For example, **go ahead and try** these two commands, and compare their output:

```
Get-Process | Where Name -like "s*" | Format-List

Get-Process | Format-List | Where Name -like "s*"
```

See the difference? The second command won't really work, because by the time the `Where` command runs, you don't have `Process` objects anymore. There's no `Name` column to look for s* in. In the second command, we've made a key mistake of attempting to "work with" those proprietary text-display structures, and it just won't work. This reinforces the fact that **once you format something, you're done**.

This can get especially confusing for PowerShell newcomers, because these two commands will seem to do basically the same thing:

```
Get-Process | Select -Property Name,Id

Get-Process | Format-Table -Property Name,Id
```

The `Select` command (really, `Select-Object`, but we're using the friendlier-sounding alias) takes objects and trims off all but the properties, or "columns," that you specify. Its output goes to the pipeline, which secretly goes to `Out-Default`, which goes to `Out-Host`, which calls the formatting system. Because we've stripped off most of the properties, the pre-defined formatting view we've seen previously will no longer work. PowerShell sees that there are 2 properties, which is less than 5, and so it constructs a table.

In the second example, we've gone straight to the formatting system, and told it explicitly to construct a table with just two columns. So what's the difference?

In the second example, **we're done**. We can't really tack on any other commands, except for a couple of `Out-` commands (like `Out-File`) that specifically understand the proprietary text-display structures. In the first example, however, we could have added more commands, because `Select` is still producing structured data *objects*.

Try These

We'd like you to try the following, just so you can start to get a personal idea of how all this works, and what the possibilities are. These will work in both Windows PowerShell and PowerShell Core, and they'll work in any version of either.

1. Using `Get-Process` and `Get-Member`, make a list of all the properties, or "columns," generated by `Get-Process`. You'll use this list in the next steps.
2. Can you force PowerShell to create a table that includes 8 of the properties (you choose which ones)?
3. Can you have the shell create a list display that only includes the `Name` and `Id` properties? We showed you `Format-Table`, which produces tables; what command might produce lists?
4. We gave you a hint to this: can you have the default output of `Get-Process` go to a text file?

We're very deliberately not going to give you an "answer key" to these tasks, because it's important that you figure them out on your own. If you get really stuck, hop on the forums on PowerShell.org and ask for help, but it's worth spending a good chunk of time trying to get these to work on your own.

Messing with Objects

We've introduced you to a couple of object-manipulation commands in this chapter, but we wanted to provide a more complete list. Try running `Get-Command -Noun Object` to see what commands, other than these, the shell offers. Here are some key ones:

- The `Where-Object` command takes a bunch of objects, and using criteria you specify, removes some of them from the pipeline. Only the objects that meet your criteria get "passed on" to the next command in the pipeline. Think of this command as *choosing which rows get kept.*
- The `Select-Object` lets you specify the properties you want passed down the pipeline. It actually "consumes" the objects you pipe in, and creates new objects to pipe out. Those new objects won't necessarily have the same type name as the ones you piped in (which means the text output might look different, since the formatting system will follow different rules). Think of this command as *choosing which columns get kept.*
- The `Measure-Object` command counts up the objects you pipe in, and it outputs an object containing that number. You can also ask it to look at a single numeric property and produce a sum, minimum value, and maximum value for that property.
- The `Sort-Object` command reorders the objects you give it based on the values in one or more columns. It sorts in ascending order by default.

Spend a few moments reviewing the help files for these commands, because they're going to be incredibly useful to you as you move forward with PowerShell. And, more importantly, **spend some time "playing" with these commands, perhaps by piping `Get-Process` to them**. You're not going to hurt anything on your computer, and some unstructured "play time" will let you experiment, and start building your own mental model of how these commands work and what they can do for you.

PowerShell Plays Along

PowerShell has a slightly annoying "feature" that we want you to be aware of. Try this - and be very careful with the typing, as we've introduced a deliberate typo that we want you to duplicate:

```
Get-Process | Select -Property Nmae,Id
```

What did you get?

PowerShell tends to assume that you're smarter than it. When you asked it to display a property called "Nmae," PowerShell didn't think, "this person is crazy, there's no such thing." It just assumed you wanted a property named "Nmae" for some reason (those crazy humans, are we right?), and so it did. It didn't have any data to put *in* that column, so you just got a blank property. You can confirm this by running this:

```
Get-Process | Select -Property Nmae,Id | Get-Member
```

See? Like we wrote earlier `Select` is constructing an all-new object, and in this case it's got an `Nmae` property, just like you told it to. There actually *are* some beneficial reasons for this behavior, as there are some advanced tricks you can use to create and populate new properties on-the-fly, but *mostly* this behavior just trips up newcomers who aren't careful when they type.

Objects: the Important Bits

Remember that *objects* are just what we call the structured data that most PowerShell commands produce.

Objects usually represent something on your computer, like a running process, a file, a user account, and so on. Try using `Get-ChildItem` instead of `Get-Process` in some of the examples we've covered in this chapter.

Objects have *properties*, which you can think of as the columns in a table, where each object is a row in that table.

Objects have a *type name* that uniquely identifies the *kind* of structure they are. Various PowerShell systems use that type name to engage different behaviors on a per-type basis.

A few PowerShell commands don't output objects, and that includes the `Format-` commands. Once you hand objects off to these commands, the objects are "consumed," and you can't work with them anymore.

9. Enter the Pipeline

For operating system command-line shells, pipelines are nothing new. Some of the oldest shells out there, mostly associated with Unix systems, have had pipelining. It looks a little like this:

```
ps -ef | grep httpd
```

That first command, in Unix or Linux, would retrieve a list of running processes on the system. Traditional shell commands send all of their output to a special "stream" called *stdout*, or "standard out." It's really just a way for the command to tell the operating system what to display, a bit like you putting papers in an "out basket" on your desk when you're done with them and want someone to take them away. Normally, the operating system takes whatever text is in stdout and displays it on the screen.

> But the *vertical pipe character*, or `|`, tells the operating system to take whatever is in the first command's stdout and stick it in the second command's *stdin*. "Standard in," as you might guess, is where commands get their input. So the pipeline is taking whatever `ps` output, and feeding it to `grep`. The `grep` command, in Linux and Unix, is used to filter through text output by looking for specific text strings, like "httpd."

Traditional shells, with their text-based command output, use this pattern *a lot*. Most of the time, working in these shells consists of (a) figuring out which command will produce the data you need, and (b) figuring out how to parse the data you need out of all the other text the command is producing. Because every command's output is different, you spend a lot of time "piping" to text-parsing commands, and a lot of time figuring out how to make those text-parsing commands do what you want. For experienced shell users, this is almost second nature, but for newcomers it can be a pretty steep learning curve.

PowerShell works a little differently.

Six Pipelines

In actuality, a PowerShell command can stick output into as many as *six* "out baskets." PowerShell doesn't have stdout or stdin. Instead, for output, it supports six pipeline "streams":

- **Success**. This is the closest to stdout; it's the "main" pipeline, and it's where the command's usual output goes. That output isn't text, though—as you learned in the previous chapter, it's all objects when it hits the pipeline.
- **Error**. Errors are written to this pipeline. Traditional shells, in addition to stdin and stdout, also support stderr, or "standard error." That's similar to PowerShell's error pipeline, although the error pipeline also contains objects, not text.
- **Verbose**. When a command wants to generate some text to let you know what it's doing, it can send that text to this pipeline. This pipeline, like the others, can be

suppressed, so if you don't want the verbose output to be displayed, you can shut it off. It's actually off by default; running any command with the `-Verbose` parameter will turn it on for that command. Traditional shell commands often supported a "verbose mode," but when you used it, the verbose output went to stdout along with the command's normal output, making things a bit confusing to parse.
- **Warning**. When something's not as serious as an error, PowerShell commands can output text information to this pipeline.
- **Debug**. A special pipeline, enabled by running the command with the `-Debug` parameter, can enable debugging modes in commands that support it.
- **Informational**. Introduced in PowerShell 5, this pipeline provides a way to log structured data about the command's performance. This is a little like the Verbose pipeline, only output can be tagged and categorized, making it easier to sort through later, if needed.

So how do you use these six pipelines? We're going to focus on the first and most important one: success.

Simple Pipeline Examples

Consider this one:

```
Get-Process | Where Name -like "*s*"
```

This will display all running processes whose names contain the letter `s`; the `-like` operator supports *wildcard matches*, and the * wildcard means "any zero or more characters." `Where` is an alias to the `Where-Object` command. And actually, that syntax is a little bit of a shortcut. In the next chapter, we'll dig into a bit more. For now, let's focus on how data is traveling from one command to the other.

If we run:

```
Get-Process | Get-Member
```

We can see that `Get-Process` is producing objects of the type `System.Diagnostics.Process`. Those are being dumped into the Success pipeline, and the vertical pipe character is asking PowerShell to hand those to the next command. But since PowerShell command's don't have the stdin of traditional shells, where exactly is PowerShell "sticking" those objects?

Here's a simple rule that leads to a complex topic: **All PowerShell commands receive their input from parameters, and only from parameters**. Anytime you think, "nah, there's something else happening," you're wrong; PowerShell might be doing something invisible behind the scenes, but it's still using parameters.

You're hopefully used to parameters by now. For example:

```
Get-Process -Name *s*
```

That'll also display all processes with the letter `s` in their name. The `-Name` parameter of that particular command accepts wildcards (the help file says so). So when we run:

```
Get-Process | Where Name -like "*s*"
```

Which parameter of `Where-Object` is the output of `Get-Process` being attached to? It'd be easy to imagine that every PowerShell command has some secret parameter for receiving pipeline input, but that's not the case. Every single command makes its own decisions about accepting pipeline input. Some commands don't accept it at all; others can accept it in a variety of ways.

Pipeline Input: Plan A

PowerShell has two ways of sending objects from one command to another, and the first way it *always* tries is called "ByValue." We already had `Get-Member` tell us that `Get-Process` produces objects of the type `System.Diagnostics.Process`. ByValue simply tries to find a parameter that wants that same type. Have a look at the full help file for `Where-Object`[1]. Do you see a parameter that accepts objects of the type `System.Diagnostics.Process`?

We don't. We see `PSObject`, we see `String`, we see others, but we don't see that one. But hang on: there's a trick. All objects are technical specialized versions of `System.Object`, or just `Object`. So parameters that accept a data type of `Object` or `PSObject` (which is "PowerShell object") can technically accept *anything*, like being a universal blood recipient. So now we have two "candidate" parameters: `-InputObject`, which accepts `PSObject`, and `-Value`, which accepts `Object`. If you scroll down a bit in the help file to those parameters, you'll see:

---

[1]pulluphttps://docs.microsoft.com/en-us/powershell/module/microsoft.powershell.core/where-object?view=powershell-6

```
    -InputObject <psobject>

        Required?                    false
        Position?                    Named
        Accept pipeline input?       true (ByValue)
        Parameter set name           (All)
        Aliases                      None
        Dynamic?                     false

     -Value <Object>

        Required?                    false
        Position?                    1
        Accept pipeline input?       false
        Parameter set name           ContainsSet, C\
ase...
```

So the `-Value` parameter *doesn't accept pipeline input.* So we don't even need to worry about that one. The `-InputObject` parameter does, though, and it specifically accepts it "ByValue," which is the plan we're working with right now.

And so, very simply, whatever comes out of `Get-Process` will get stuck to the `-InputObject` parameter of `Where-Object`. What the command does with it from there is up to it; PowerShell is just concerned with getting the objects from point A to point B, and that job is done.

PowerShell will *always* try to do ByValue first, because it lets it send the entire object from one command to the next. Now, you might ask, "yeah, but what if `Where-Object` had two parameters, both of which accepted `Object`, and both of which accepted pipeline input ByValue? Which would PowerShell choose?" Well the fact is, *commands aren't allowed to do that.*

It's illegal. A command can only define *one* parameter to accept a given object type from the pipeline ByValue (there's a variation called *parameter sets* that can seem to bypass this rule, but it's a bit complex so we won't go into it here).

But what if PowerShell is trying to pass objects along and no parameter is capable of receiving them ByValue?

Pipeline Input: Plan B

Plan B for pipeline input is called "ByPropertyName," and it happens only if PowerShell can't figure out what to do with ByValue (and incidentally, if ByPropertyName also fails, PowerShell will generate an error and stop running the commands). To illustrate how this works, we're going to create a Comma-Separated Values (CSV) file, using a basic text editor.

```
Name
pwsh
bash
httpd
```

We realize this doesn't actually have any commas in it, but we only need to define one column. We've made a `Name` column, which contains three values.

Now, in PowerShell, we'll use the `Import-CSV` command to read in that file. It's designed to create an object from each data row, so we'll have three objects. For each object, the columns (in our case, just a singular column) become properties:

```
PS /Users/donjones> import-csv test.csv           \


Name
----
pwsh
bash
httpd
```

Cool. Let's run that to `Get-Member` and see what the type name is:

```
PS /Users/donjones> import-csv test.csv |
Get-Member

TypeName: System.Management.Automation.PSCustomObje\
ct

Name        MemberType   Definition
----        ----------   ----------
Equals      Method       bool Equals(...
GetHashCode Method       int GetHashCode()
GetType     Method       type GetType()
ToString    Method       string ToString()
Name        NoteProperty string Name=pwsh
```

So we've got a `PSCustomObject`, and we can see that it does indeed have a Name property. The other members are methods, and they're built into the base `Object` type that this was made from.

Have a look at the help for `Get-Process`[2]. Do you see a param-

[2]ahttps://docs.microsoft.com/en-us/powershell/module/microsoft.powershell.management/get-process?view=powershell-6

eter capable of accepting `PSCustomObject` ByValue from the pipeline? No? Well, there goes Plan A! On to Plan B. With Plan B, we're looking for parameters that accept pipeline input ByPropertyName. We're seeing `-Id` and `-Name`. So given those two parameters as "candidates," we ask ourselves:

Does our object have an Id property? No, the `Get-Member` output doesn't show one. So forget that one. Does our object have. Name property? Yes it does! So here's the magic, which is so low-tech that it's easy to to believe in it: because the `-Name` parameter and the Name property *are spelled the same*, the values from our Name property will attach to the `-Name` parameter. PowerShell would actually be happy to "attach" as many matching properties as we had, but we only gave it Name.

So we're going to run this:

```
Import-Csv test.csv | Get-Process
```

And in essence, we're telling PowerShell to do this:

```
Get-Process -Name pwsh
Get-Process -Name bash
Get-Process -Name httpd
```

Because those are the values in our CSV file. Let's do it:

```
PS /Users/donjones> import-csv test.csv | get-proce\
ss

 NPM(K)    PM(M)      WS(M)     CPU(s)      Id
 ------    -----      -----     ------      --
      0     0.00      69.73     446.36   27168
      0     0.00       1.67       2.79   27149
get-process : Cannot find a process with the name "\
httpd". Verify the process name and call the cmdlet\
 again.
At line:1 char:23
+ import-csv test.csv | get-process
+                       ~~~~~~~~~~~
+ CategoryInfo          : ObjectNotFound: (httpd:St\
ring) [Get-Process], ProcessCommandException
+ FullyQualifiedErrorId : NoProcessFoundForGivenNam\
e,Microsoft.PowerShell.Commands.GetProcessCommand
```

Two of them worked, while the third, `httpd`, generated an error, because we apparently don't have a process with that name running on our system. That's cool, because it means our command still worked.

Re-read this a few times, if you need to, to make sure you understand it. It's a powerful technique, and knowing *why* it works is critical to using it yourself going forward.

Wrapping Up

With traditional shells' support for a single stdout and stdin, and with traditional commands' exclusive use of text for output and input, pipelining was easy to understand, but could be difficult to master. In PowerShell, you've really still got one main "path" between commands, but they're passing structured data known as *objects*. That gives PowerShell some options when piping objects, and it uses two techniques—ByValue and ByPropertyName—to do it.

10. Filtering and Selecting

PowerShell's `-Object` commands, designed to work with anything you can chuck into the pipeline, enable some of its most useful and powerful capabilities. In this chapter, we'll focus on two key ones: filtering and selecting.

Filtering

Filtering is when you specify some kind of logical criteria, and PowerShell removes some objects from the pipeline which don't meet your criteria. Objects that do meet your criteria continue on the pipeline to whatever command is next. Or, if there are no more commands, those "matching" objects are the ones you end up seeing in the final output.

Consider this:

```
Get-Process | Where Name -like "*s*"
```

This will display all running processes whose names contain the letter `s`; the `-like` operator supports *wildcard matches*, and the `*` wildcard means "any zero or more characters." `Where` is an alias to the `Where-Object` command. And actually, that syntax is a little bit of a shortcut. We're using two parameters positionally; if we went full-on with the syntax, it would look like this:

```
Get-Process | Where-Object -Property Name -like -Va\
lue "*s*"
```

That's perhaps "more correct" from a syntax perspective, but it doesn't "read" as much like an English statement. The command also has an older (and still very useful) syntax:

```
Get-Process | Where-Object -FilterScript { $_.Name \
-like "*s*" }
```

You'll often see this with `-FilterScript` omitted, and the { script block } provided positionally:

```
Get-Process | Where { $_.Name -like "*s*" }
```

Here's what's happening: those {curly brackets} denote an actual PowerShell script, albeit a wee little one. Within those brackets, `Where-Object` has been programmed to compare the current pipeline object, represented by $_, to the literal string `"*s*"`. The comparison operator in use, `-like`, is a *wildcard comparison.* So it reads the `*` characters as standing for any "zero or more characters." So this expression would match words like `svchost`, `process`, and `dnssvc`, because each of those contains `s`, preceded or followed by zero or more other characters. Try it out!

Other comparison operators include:

- The basic operators such as `-eq` for equality, `-ne` for inequality, `-gt` for greater than, `-lt` for less than, and `-gte` or `-lte` for greater than or equal to and less than or equal to. For string comparisons, these are all case-insensitive.

- The `-like` and `-notlike` wildcard operators.
- The `-match` and `-notmatch` operators, which are like super-charged wildcard operators. These operate using *regular expressions*, which is a powerful string-comparison language (that's beyond the scope of this book).

Be wary of the `-in`, `-notin`, `-contains`, and `-notcontains` operators. It can be easy to read something like:

```
$_.Name -contains "s"
```

And think, "yeah, that'll check to see if the Name property has an 's' in it." But nope. Those four operators are designed to work against collections and arrays, and although the above "reads" correctly in English, it's not how PowerShell sees it. Stick with `-like` when you need to make a wildcard comparison like that.

Now there's a bit of confusion that newcomers run into with `$_`. "Where the heck did that come from?" you might wonder. Let us explain. Take a look at this example, *which will not work correctly*, and try to think about it from PowerShell's point of view:

```
Get-User | Where { Name -like "*Jason*" }
```

PowerShell sees this and says, "Okay, I'm going to get a bunch of user accounts. Cool. I'm going to pipe those to `Where-Object`, which is going to keep... hmm. I'm only supposed to keep things with a Name like 'Jason,' but *whose* name? Your name? The computer's name? The President's name?" You see, PowerShell doesn't *know* that you're trying to work with the objects that were piped in. So `$_` was created as a generic way of referring to "whatever was piped in." It's *very important* to know that `$_` will only work in special situations where PowerShell has been preprogrammed to *look for* `$_`, and `Where-Object`'s filter script happens to be one of those places (there are about half a dozen or so "special" places, and we'll point them out as we come to them). You can also use `$PSItem` in place of `$_` if you find that easier to read, although you'll tend to see most people using `$_` since that's the one PowerShell started with in v1.

We tend to think of `$_` as a fill-in-the-blank form field, like on a tax form.

```
Enter your income: ________
Send in the full amount. Thank you.
```

See, the underline is where you fill-in your information, right? So `$_` uses an underline, because PowerShell is meant to "fill in" with a piped-in object. The `$_.Name` syntax means, "I don't want to look at the *entire* piped-in object; I only want to look at the `Name` property."

`Where-Object` can also handle multiple comparisons, but it can only do so if you use the { filter script } syntax. For example:

```
Get-Process |
Where { $_.Name -like '*s*' -and $_.Name -notlike '\
*d*' }
```

This will list processes which contain "s" in their name, but not "d." This syntax also throws newcomers a lot of the time. You'll see people try this, which won't work:

```
Get-Process |
Where { $_.Name -like '*s*' -and -notlike '*d*' }
```

As humans, we get what you might mean by this, but PowerShell doesn't. You see, the two expressions on either side of `-and` (and this applies to `-or` as well) must be complete. *Complete* means that each expression must have two *operands* on other side of the operator. Sometimes, it can help to visually group the expressions by using parentheses:

```
Get-Process |
Where { ($_.Name -like '*s*') -and (-notlike '*d*')\
 }
```

You can easily see that the second set of parentheses contains only an operator and one operand; it needs *two* operands to be valid:

```
Get-Process |
Where { ($_.Name -like '*s*') -and ($_.Name -notlik\
e '*d*') }
```

Give that last one a try and see what it does on your computer. As a note, you can type it exactly as we've shown here, hitting Return after the vertical pipe character. PowerShell will enter a kind of "extended prompt" mode, and you just hit Return on a blank prompt when you've finished typing. That signals to the shell that you're done, and it'll execute everything you've typed.

Being Efficient with Filtering

There's something else we need to tell you about filtering, before we move on. While `Where-Object` is a great general-purpose filter-er, it can sometimes be slow. Consider this:

```
Get-GroceryStore | Where { $_.Type -eq 'Apple' }
```

This is akin to sending someone to *buy an entire grocery store*, bring it home, and then sort through the trucks until you get all the apples out. You just throw the rest of the food in the trash. Not very efficient, is it? Anytime a PowerShell command is returning hundreds of objects (or more), this filtering approach can be slow and wasteful.

Instead, *some* PowerShell commands have their own filtering built right in. For example, these two commands will do the same thing:

```
Get-Process -Name s*

Get-Process | Where Name -like "s*"
```

In this case, `Get-Process` happens to have its own filtering capability, so long as the Name property is what you want to filter on. Asking the command to do this filtering will run much more quickly, since PowerShell won't be "buying the entire grocery store" and then sorting just for the apples—the command will only be returning the things you wanted in the first place. Kind of like this:

```
Get-GroceryStore -Filter "/produce/apple"
```

Now, the downside of using a command's built-in filtering is that, as shown in the above example, each command gets to define its own filtering syntax. Often times, you can't use PowerShell operators such as `-like` or `-eq`; instead, you have to learn whatever filtering the command wants you to use. That means a bit of extra learning burden on you, in exchange for faster and more efficient filtering. You can usually read the command's help file to see examples of how it wants you to specify filtering criteria.

Selecting Properties

If you remember from the chapter on formatting, PowerShell has some rules for displaying command's output objects. In many cases, one of PowerShell's configuration files will specify a default *view*, which details the properties that PowerShell should display. You've also learned that PowerShell's `Format-` commands allow you to override those defaults, and construct whatever custom lists or tables you want. But you *also* learned that the `Format-` commands basically discard the original objects, leaving you with formatting directives that can't be used for much beyond text file or on-screen output. For example, try this:

```
Get-Process |
Format-Table Name,Id |
ConvertTo-HTML |
Out-File process-test.html
```

Now open the resulting HTML file in your web browser and enjoy the ugly. So how could you make this work the way you intended? `Select-Object` (or its alias, `Select`) is the answer.

```
Get-Process |
Select-Object Name,Id |
ConvertTo-HTML |
Out-File process-test.html
```

Unlike `Format-` commands, which are designed to create attractively formatted output for screens and text files, the `Select-Object` command isn't producing formatting directives. Instead, `Select` is producing a new object that has only the properties you specified—`Name and` Id‘ in this case. The resulting objects *are still objects*, and can be piped to pretty much any other PowerShell command that can work with them. Give the above example a try, and notice the difference when you open the new HTML file in your browser.

Advanced Selecting

Check this out—it may blow your mind a bit, but we'll explain each piece.

```
Get-Process |
Select-Object Name,Id,@{name='Proc';expression={$_.\
cpu}} |
ConvertTo-HTML |
Out-File process-test.html
```

Try it—go ahead and run that, look at the HTML in a web browser, and then come back here for the explanation.

Most of that command should look familiar, because it's the same command we ran in the previous section. There's only one new bit:

```
@{name='Proc';expression={$_.cpu}}
```

So, this new bit showed up in the property list of the `Select-Object`. That means *we're actually creating a brand-new property* for each object in the pipeline. This structure is called a *hash table*, which consists of **name=value** pairs. You can see that this hash table includes two such pairs, named `name` and `expression`. You see, `Select-Object` has been specially programmed to understand hash tables containing pairs with these names (the `Format-` commands do, also). The command takes the `name` pair and creates a new property having that name—"Proc," in this instance. To fill in the value for the new property, the command looks at the `expression`. The expression itself is a {script block}, not unlike the filter script that `Where-Object` can use. And, like `Where-Object`, this script block can use `$_` (or `$PSItem`) to refer to "whatever object was piped in."

In this case, we're taking the Process objects' native CPU property, and basically adding a new property called "Proc" which will contain the CPU value. This is one way to create custom-looking output if you don't like one of the objects' built-in property names.

Wrapping Up

This chapter was meant to get you started with the various `-Object` commands by showing you the two most common ones, and helping you understand the pattern of piping objects from one command to another. Run this:

```
Get-Command -Noun Object
```

To see other "generic" commands that can be incredibly useful. Read their help files to understand what they do, and to see some examples of how they work.

11. The Very Basics of Scripting

People tend to make a big deal of scripting, as if it requires some kind of advanced computer science degree. It doesn't. Think of a script as being very similar to the ones they use in Hollywood: it's a list of instructions that the actors are to follow. Scripts include actions for the actors, like "pick up a pot," as well as lines of dialogue to recite. PowerShell scripts are basically just like that, only they tell a *computer* what to do, instead of a human actor.

Consider the following command, which will only typically work on Windows-based systems:

```
Get-CimInstance -ClassName Win32_OperatingSystem `
 -ComputerName SERVER1
```

This tells PowerShell to use its Common Information Model (CIM) system to retrieve the CIM class known as "Win32_OperatingSystem" from a computer named SERVER1. That class provides information about the computer's installed operating system. It's a useful enough command, and it's one you could conceivably share with other people on your team.

All you'd have to do is type that into a text file, make sure the file had a `.ps1` filename extension, and you could run it as-is right in PowerShell. For example, suppose you saved it as `Get-OSInfo.ps1`; you'd just run:

```
PS C:\> ./Get-OSInfo.ps1
```

PowerShell requires that scripts be run from a path; in this case, the path `./` refers to the current directory. Assuming `Get-OSInfo.ps1` is in the current directory (which is `C:\`, according to the prompt), it'll run.

But the script has limited usefulness, because it's *hardcoded* to a particular remote computer name, right? Sure, you could just tell your colleagues, "look, whenever you want to query a different computer, just open the file in Notepad and change the computer name. I mean, don't change the part that actually says `-ComputerName`, change the name `SERVER1` to something else."

Someone's gonna screw that up.

A better approach would be to *parameterize* the script:

```
Param(
 $x
)
Get-CimInstance -ClassName Win32_OperatingSystem `
 -ComputerName $x
```

This creates an *input parameter* so that someone can specify a new remote computer name each time they run the script, without having to edit the script. The `Param` block is a comma-separated list of input parameters. Whatever values are provided to those are stored in variables, which you can then use within the script. So `$x` stores the computer name the user is trying to reach, and you can see where we've used it in lieu of a hardcoded computer name. You'd run the script like this, now:

```
PS C:\> ./Get-OSInfo.ps1 -x SERVER2
```

See, the `$x` parameter in the script gets used just like a "real" PowerShell command parameter, `-x`. Although honestly, looking at it now, "x" seems like a stupid name. It's not very intuitive. Most PowerShell commands that accept a computer name do so by using a `-ComputerName` parameter, and we should probably be consistent with that:

```
Param(
 $ComputerName
)
Get-CimInstance -ClassName Win32_OperatingSystem `
 -ComputerName $ComputerName
```

See, we changed the *definition* of our parameter, in the `Param` block, as well as the *usage* of our parameter, in the `Get-CimInstance` command. To run this:

```
PS C:\> ./Get-OSInfo.ps1 -ComputerName SERVER2
```

Although come to think of it, people are likely to just run it without the parameter, which would probably cause an error. We can make sure they provide a value:

```
Param
 [Parameter(Mandatory=$True)]$ComputerName
)
Get-CimInstance -ClassName Win32_OperatingSystem `
 -ComputerName $ComputerName
```

There, that's better. And honestly, that's just about all there is to it! This script is what we call a *controller*, in that it isn't creating any new functionality, but is instead making it a bit easier to access a given piece of functionality. Controller scripts typically just combine a bunch of commands that you, or someone else (like Microsoft) have written, ensuring the commands run in the right order and that all the right parameter values are provided.

It's also entirely possible to *write your very own commands* in PowerShell, and it's a great way to add new functionality to the shell. That topic is a bit beyond this book's scope, though; we suggest getting into *Learn PowerShell Scripting in a Month of Lunches* if you want to tackle that more-advanced topic.

Wrapping Up

Getting into scripting–especially "the right way," as we've outlined in this chapter–is truly how you take your PowerShell skills to "the next level." It's how you move from solving one-off problems to becoming a true automation machine!

12. Going Remote

One cool thing PowerShell offers (and has since v2) is *Remoting*. Basically, Remoting lets you send commands to a remote computer, which also runs PowerShell, and have the remote computer execute those commands. It then sends the results back to you. This chapter will offer a quick intro to Remoting; there's a *lot* of technical details we'll gloss over, but you can find those in the free ebook, *Secrets of PowerShell Remoting*, available at https://leanpub.com/secretsofpowershellremoting.

Enabling Remoting

In *Windows* PowerShell, you'll find Remoting enabled by default on server operating systems (e.g., Windows Server). You have to manually enable it on client operating systems by running `Enable-PSRemoting`. For *PowerShell*–e.g., PowerShell "Core" that runs on macOS, Windows, and Linux–you'll usually need to make some decisions about the kind of connectivity you want to use. Head over to the official documentation[1] to read up on it.

Connectivity

PowerShell uses its own protocol to "talk" to remote copies of itself. That protocol is called MS-PSRP, or Microsoft PowerShell Remoting Protocol.

---

[1]https://docs.microsoft.com/en-us/powershell/scripting/core-powershell/running-remote-commands?view=powershell-6

PSRP, as its friends call it, can physically connect to the network using two different lower-level protocols. One option, which is the original one and the most-used in all-Windows networks, is Web Services for Management, or WS-MAN. Microsoft implements this protocol in a service called Windows Remote Management, or WinRM; that's the actual piece of software that knows how to "talk" WS-MAN. On Windows machines, `Enable-PSRemoting` will configure WinRM automagically. Another options, available in PowerShell v6 and later, is to use Secure Shell, or SSH, to convey PSRP across the network. SSH is the preferred option on mixed-OS networks, although getting it set up can require a bit of extra work (the docs we reference above have instructions).

Since this book is targeted at newbies, we're going to assume that the tricky setup bits are already done in your environment. This also isn't intended to be an exhaustive look at Remoting; the *Secrets* book we referenced earlier goes into the gory details, including the security mechanisms that Remoting uses in different situations.

Sending Remote Commands

The main command you'll use with Remoting is `Invoke-Command`. It offers two options: you an send a *script block* containing one or more commands to transmit, or you can give it a `-FilePath` to a script that lives on your local computer. In the latter case, the script file will be opened locally, and the *contents* transmitted to the remote machine. That means you can send complex scripts without the remote machine actually needing physical access to the script file. For now, though, we're going to play with the first option: a script block.

```
Invoke-Command -ComputerName ONE,TWO,THREE `
-ScriptBlock {
 Get-Process -Name s* |
 Where CPU -gt 10
}
```

This is going to send our script block to *three* computers, named ONE, TWO, and THREE. The presumption is that something on your network, such as a DNS server, will know how to translate those computer names into IP addresses. The other presumption is that the person running all this is (a) permitted to remotely connect to each of these computers, and (b) permitted to run that command on those computers. On an all-Windows network where all three computers, and the computer kicking this all off, are in the same domain, this will "just work." Again, we're going to assume you're in an environment where this has all been set up already, so you don't need to worry (for now) about the gory details.

There's something important to notice about the way we ran that command, and to really make the point, we're going to provide an alternative:

```
Invoke-Command -ComputerName ONE,TWO,THREE `
-ScriptBlock {
 Get-Process -Name s*
} |
Where CPU -gt 10
```

See the difference?

In the first example, the remote computers are each getting all the processes whose names start with `s`, and they're then filtering it so that we only see processes whose CPU time is greater than 10 seconds. Each computer will then transmit the results back to us. PowerShell conveniently adds a `PSComputerName` property to each result we get back, so we can tell which of the three computers each result came from.

In the second example, the remote computers are each getting all of the processes whose names start with `s`, just as before. But *that* is what they're sending back. So we're getting potentially more information back, and then we're *locally* filtering the results down to just those whose CPU time exceeds 10 seconds. That potentially means our local computer doing a lot more work, and it potentially means a lot more data being sent across the network. The first example is likely going to be more efficient in some cases. That's a big thing to remember in Remoting: *where is the work being done?*

Remote Jobs

Sometimes, you may need to send long-running, complex commands to remote computers, and you might not want to hang around and wait for the results to come in. In those situations, you can add the `-AsJob` parameter to `Invoke-Command`, and it will run everything on a background thread. You can then run `Get-Job` to check the job status, and `Receive-Job` to retrieve the final results, once they're in. The job is "co-ordinated" by your local computer, and you need to leave PowerShell running so the remote results will have something to "come back to." Once you close your local shell, the job is essentially terminated.

Wrapping Up

As we said, we wanted this to be a short introduction to Remoting. It's a big, complex topic, and you can do a *lot* with it. Now that you know it exists, and you know it's core capability, you can start exploring it more on your own.

13. Understanding Your OS

When you drive a modern car, you don't need to know much about it. The car's various controls and instruments remove you from much of the under-the-hood workings. In science terms, the car *abstracts* you from the mechanics of the car. When you want it to "go," you stomp on the accelerator, without worrying about the terrifically complex mechanics that actually result in forward motion.

PowerShell is a little like driving a car that has no dashboard, no pedals, no transmission shifter, and no steering wheel. That is, it doesn't provide very much *abstraction* on top of the operating system or whatever other technology product you're trying to mess with. If you want the car to "go," you need to know exactly which two wires need exactly how much voltage applied across them in order to correctly signal the car's controller computer; too much or too little, and you could cause a major crash. Same thing with PowerShell. You're tinkering with the computer's brains, and if you're a little off, you could lobotomize the whole thing.

In the forums on PowerShell.org (where you're welcome to join us), we're constantly fielding questions that often have little to do with PowerShell itself, and more to do with the underlying technology. We still try and answer when we can, but it's sometimes hard. For example:

```
New-ADUser -Name Joe
```

Will that create a new Active Directory user named "Joe?" *Maybe.* In most environments, it'll work, but if you use the same syntax to try and create a user named "Jane," it'll fail. Why? Well, it's not a PowerShell problem. You see, all Active Directory users are required to have a unique Security Account Manager (SAM) name, called the samAccountName. But we didn't provide one. So the first user, Joe, got created with a blank samAccountName—something surprisingly legal in Active Directory, although if you're doing this in their Graphical User Interface (GUI) it *abstracts* you away from the underlying bits enough to not allow it. Creating Jane fails because a "blank" samAccountName is no longer unique—Joe has one. Again, not a PowerShell problem *per se*, but a problem you'd only run into *in* PowerShell. Ultimately, the cause in most cases is *you don't know the product as well as you think you do*, in many cases because a GUI has been abstracting away the hard stuff on you all this time.

So the real difficulty in using PowerShell is that it exposes you to all the weird, underlying goofiness in whatever software or operating system stuff you're messing with. It means that to use PowerShell effectively, you need to be, or become, a real *master* of your trade. There's no book that can give you that, but there are steps you can take.

- **Experience**. People tend to think *experience* means *time*, but it doesn't. Experience actually means *failing and figuring it out.* The more times you fail and figure it out, the more experienced you are. The problem is that people hate failing so much they actively try to avoid it, which means they're actively preventing themselves from becoming experienced. Invest in a virtualization product (like VMware or Parallels) so you can run a "lab" virtual machine on your computer. Experiment—and fail—in that virtual machine.

- **Understanding**. Way too many people—and we mean a *lot*—just want an answer handed to them, which they then try to mangle into their own version to meet their immediate need. This is not learning, it is mimicking. Even if someone is kind enough to answer one of your questions with a full answer, stop and take the time to *understand* it. If you don't know *why* they said what they said, politely ask. Express your desire to *understand*, so that you never have to ask that question again. If you can't explain, to someone else, *why* that answer is the answer, then you're not learning.
- **Troubleshooting**. This is another place where people sell themselves short. Troubleshooting isn't, "well, that didn't work, so I'll try something completely and totally different." Troubleshooting is, "well, that didn't work, so based on the evidence I'm seeing, I'll change one thing and try again." Troubleshooting it patience, and it's often slow—but it generates reliable results that you can come to understand and learn from. Too many people just don't want to take the time, in part because troubleshooting often involves multiple consecutive failures—and you now know how we feel about those.

As a note, Don's book, *How to Find a Wolf in Siberia*[a] is specifically designed to help you become a better all-purpose troubleshooter.

[a]http://leanpub.com/troubleshooting

So as you become stuck in PowerShell—and if you're doing it right, you *will* become stuck, eventually—take the time to *figure it out.* Ask for help in online forums like PowerShell.org and StackOverflow.com. Explain what you're trying to do, what you've tried, and what the results were (error messages and *short* code snippets are invaluable). Read the answer, and make sure you *understand* it. Apply that understanding to your next problem, and start engaging in troubleshooting.

But understand that, along the way, you're really going to be learning more about the technologies you're working with than you are about PowerShell itself. That's good! PowerShell is just a tool; the stuff you're using it with is where the real adventure awaits.

14. The Chapter of Gotchas

This chapter is designed to help get you through some of PowerShell's most irritating "gotchas." The ones that tend to trip up newcomers the most. The ones that most make you want to slam your head into your desk. There are more that we'll cover here, though, and we want to strongly recommend *The Big Book of PowerShell Gotchas*, which is available for free at https://leanpub.com/thebigbookofpowershellgotchas.

Format to the Right

In the chapter on formatting, we tried to help you understand why this won't work:

```
Get-Process |
Format-Table -Prop Name,Id,CPU |
ConvertTo-HTML
```

Formatting commands, such as `Format-Table`, *consume* the objects piped to them and emit specialized formatting directives. Those directives can pretty much be used only to construct a nicely formatted screen display, or an equivalent-looking text file. We therefore use the memory aid, "format right," meaning, "get the formatting command all the way to the end, or to the right, of the command." Once you format something, you're *done*; you shouldn't expect to pipe that on to anything else.

"But how can I pick what properties I want to output without using a Format command?" you may ask. Use `Select-Object` for that; formatting commands are *only* for when you're done with everything and are ready to create a prettier on-screen display.

ForEach vs. ForEach vs. ForEach

PowerShell has two distinct things, with three names, that do kinda-sorta the same thing, but differently. It gets confusing.

First, there's the `ForEach-Object` command, which has an alias, `ForEach`.

```
Get-Process |
ForEach {
 $_.Name
}
```

> This is basically the same as running `Get-Process | Select Name`. The `ForEach-Object` command, through its alias `ForEach`, is running through each object one at a time. Within its script block, the `$_` marker represents "the current piped-in object", and we're simply outputting the `Name` property of each.

There's also the *scripting construct* named `ForEach`. PowerShell uses contextual clues to figure out which one you're trying to use:

```
$processes = Get-Process
ForEach ($proc in $processes) {
 $proc.Name
 }
```

Same net output as the previous example, but a different syntax, and a slightly different execution model. Just understand that these guys all *do* the same thing at the end of the day, but they use a different syntax to get there.

Collections vs. Objects

This one is a biggie. Consider this:

```
$procs = Get-Process
```

We now have a *collection of objects* in `$procs`. *Technically*, the following doesn't make sense:

```
$procs.Name
```

That'd be like walking onto a car lot and saying, "what color is the car?" The sales guy will probably be, like, "which car, dude?" You're standing in a *collection* of cars, and you haven't referenced a *particular* car. In early versions of PowerShell, `$procs.Name` would in fact generate an error, because you're trying to get the name of a bunch of things. In current versions, however, that *will* work, and it will produce the name for every process contained in `$procs`. That's because newer versions of PowerShell *implicitly* enumerate the collection under the hood, in an attempt to do what it thinks you probably want. But that makes it more confusing when this doesn't work:

```
If ($procs.Name -like 's*') {
 $procs
 }
```

If you think about it, the comparison here makes no sense. You're saying "if the car is red, then do something" when you haven't pointed to a particular car. Technically, `$procs` isn't a process object; it's a bucket full of process objects. The bucket itself doesn't have a `Name` property; only the things *inside the bucket* do. To get at the things *inside* the bucket, you enumerate them:

```
ForEach ($proc in $procs) {
 If ($proc.Name -like 's*') {
  $proc
 }
}
```

That `ForEach` construct enumerates the collection, enabling you to work with just one of them at a time. It uses the `$proc` variable (because we told it to) to contain just one thing at a time, making it easy to work with just that one thing.

15. Where to Next?

This book was never meant to be your complete PowerShell journey. In fact, Don has an entire page[1] that kind of outlines the journey.

Our recommendation from here is to pick up a copy of *Learn Windows PowerShell in a Month of Lunches.* It's a more in-depth version of some of what's in this book, along with a *lot_more. It's got formal exercises that kind of guide you through the shell's learning journey in a deeper fashion. It's specific to _Windows* PowerShell, of course, but 90% of the book is applicable to PowerShell Core, too. You'll find it at http://Manning.com (which is the only place to buy electronic-only versions), or through Amazon and other booksellers (and all print versions contain a voucher for free electronic editions).

---

[1]http://DonJones.com/powershell

16. Welcome to the Community!

At this point, believe it or not, you no longer qualify to use the "n00b" descriptor when it comes to PowerShell. You've moved beyond that. Maybe you're no expert, but you're well on your way.

I hope you'll take this opportunity to start participating in the robust PowerShell community that's out there. Dozens of open-source projects on places like GitHub, including PowerShell Core itself, await your inspection and input. Sites like PowerShell.org need your PowerShell questions, and need you to answer questions for other people.

What's that? You're not yet far enough along to answer other people's questions? Well, with respect, bullshit. In my book, "Be the Master" (http://BeTheMaster.com), I point out that *everything you have learned* is something *someone*, somewhere, hasn't yet learned. You can help them. In fact, answering someone else's questions is one of the best ways to really cement something in your own mind, and seeing others' questions is a good excuse to try and experiment, and self-learn the answer (which you can then share with them, of course).

It's *never* to early to start participating in a community. Community is what helps turn your job into your *career*. It's where you get answers and ideas, and where you'll find your lifelong professional support mechanism. Events like

PowerShell Summit (http://powershellsummit.org) are a great way to start capitalizing on your PowerShell investment, learn new techniques, and most importantly meet your fellow Shellers face-to-face.

“Shellers” is a term I think I just made up. We’ll see how it goes.

Please don’t let this be the end of your PowerShell journey. Please let this just be the beginning. *Please* find a place online to start participating, communicating, and collaborating. Don’t be that guy or gal who only pops in to ask a question to help solve *their* problem of the moment; be the gal or guy who drops by to offer a second perspective on a question, or a first step toward an answer. If this book has helped you even a little bit, please give back to the community that helped make this book happen by *offering to help out.*

Welcome to PowerShell, and welcome to one of the warmest, friendliest global group I’ve ever been honored to be a part of. I hope you enjoy your time with us!

-Don

Made in the USA
Middletown, DE
12 October 2020

21801059R00066